WHAT REMAINS TO BE SAID

Aphorisms: New & Selected

Yahia Lababidi

WHAT REMAINS TO BE SAID

Aphorisms: New & Selected

Yahia Lababidi

wild goose publications

www.ionabooks.com

First published 2025 by
Wild Goose Publications
Suite 9, Fairfield
1048 Govan Road, Glasgow G51 4XS, Scotland
A division of Iona Community Trading CIC
Limited Company Reg. No. SC156678
www.ionabooks.com

ISBN 978-1-80432-364-9

Book design by Jane Darroch Riley

Overseas distribution
Australia: Willow Connection Pty Ltd,
1/13 Kell Mather Drive, Lennox Head NSW 2478
New Zealand: Pleroma, Higginson Street,
Otane 4170, Central Hawkes Bay

Printed in the UK by Page Bros (Norwich) Ltd

MIX
Paper | Supporting responsible forestry
FSC® C023114
FSC www.fsc.org

Preface

My first contact with Yahia Lababidi was some years ago when he submitted work to AGNI, the literary magazine I edit. Reading submissions, I look for work that freezes my reading attention and says 'Here!' Which is exactly what happened with the generous sheaf of aphorisms that Lababidi had sent. Aphorisms – we never get aphorisms. But these were, further, aphorisms of a compelling spiritual sensibility, which we likewise never see. I made my way down the page with a feeling of imminent revelation. The little awakenings came, one after the other, and I had the reader's hope that I might at any moment arrive at some unanticipated larger wakefulness.

That did not happen, quite. A series of aphorisms, however pointed or wise, can't carry a reader the full distance. That is the work of devotion and discipline. What they did accomplish, however, was important. They reminded me – and these days we all need reminding – that it is not only possible, but necessary, to find ways to speak freely of the mysteries and intimations that reveal our deep human need, a need that in our time has been sidelined by the cynical ethos of the media and our vast collective distractedness, and which draws attention, when any attention is drawn, mainly in its wispier spiritual find-your-inner-self public offerings. The aspirations of the mystical, the applications of inwardness – these have little place in our culture nowadays, and finding a way to talk openly about the soul or the revelations of beauty is very difficult. We live in the age of the eye-roll.

Which is why it was so bracing to come upon Lababidi's spiritual probes. They were not apologetic, or defensive, or shy. They addressed openly the search for meaning and a connection to forces or entities larger than the self. Keeping faith with the themes found in spiritual writings throughout history, they not only legitimised the search for deeper integration, they modelled it in a literarily compelling way. Lababidi is at once an honest and graceful writer.

I stress these things because this is the spirit that moves and fluctuates throughout Lababidi's *sui generis* gathering of meditation, memoir, social commentary, poetry, and, of course, aphorism.

I used the word 'attention' above, and I note it again here because it is a central tenet of Lababidi's thinking. He himself cites Simone Weil's well-known assertion: 'Absolute unmixed attention is prayer,' and follows its implications throughout his writing. For attention, open and directed focus, is the endangered art of giving things their due, be they objects in the outer world, or the inward stirrings we feel when we consider larger frames of reference – when we ask about meaning and purpose, and when we confront the extraordinary unlikeliness of our being here at all. Lababidi transmits on this frequency. The work is full of inklings of what might lie just beyond.

He brings together his ruminations on mysticism with compelling accounts of his own progress through stages of awareness; he searches the work of favourite writers in order to set out the connection between the literary and the transcendental. He also assesses strains of popular culture and matters of the moment. I see him as a pilgrim, and these diverse reflections show us the path of his progress.

Sven Birkerts, author, and editor of AGNI magazine

Aphorisms: New & Selected

Is it possible to master words?
Yes, in silence.

The best protection against life's corrupting experiences is innocence.

Loneliness is the price we pay
for not embracing aloneness.

Tread lightly, like someone crossing quicksand – purposefully, gingerly, like a dancer.

Like cars in amusement parks, our direction is often determined through collisions.

We cheat ourselves when we take shortcuts to vision, ecstasy or transcendence.

If we are tender with our pain, it's likely to return the favour.

Those for whom the natural is extraordinary tend to find the extraordinary natural.

The problem with celebrity culture is that the superficial external lives of strangers concern us more than our own profound inner life.

There are many ways to donate blood: writing is one.

Words of wisdom are not stolen, they are borrowed, until we make them our own.

How would we live differently
if we accepted our lives and bodies
as not our own, but on loan
from the Divine?

What we refer to as 'the real world' is often our
failure of imagination.

With enigmatic clarity,
Life gives us a different answer each time
we ask her the same question.

We can lend ideas our breath,
but ideals require our entire lives.

To anticipate the worst
is to contribute towards
its realisation.

What is considered eccentric in this world
is commonplace in another.

Each day whispers, to those who listen:
This is what is being asked of you now.

Social media: the voice that drowns out the
voice inside our head.

All languages are rough translations
of our native tongue: the Spirit.

Love calls us back
from the underworld of the self.

Detachment, paradoxically, is the ultimate
engagement – unconditional love
unconcerned with results.

We live and unlearn.

A poem is what makes you smile
when you are alone.

Fanaticism is closer to doubt than faith.

Learn to see consciousness and
conscience as one.

Free people free people.

Certain silences are harder
to take back than words.

Spiritual teachers are not prisoners
of their own time – they are free to
travel back and forth,
to better hear the past
and clearly address the future.

It is wise to know oneself, if only to add to the sum of human knowledge.

Getting older is learning to take a back seat and not insist on being interesting.

You are what you do not post online.

Pick your own battles,
not those of your culture.

What is missing from our humour is gravitas:
seriousness, intelligence, profundity,
even a tragic dimension.

Exiles are married to a dream.

When your home is on fire,
you feel the heat halfway across the world.

When we begin by taming our hearts, we also tame our tongues.

Since they make no allowances for happy surprises, cynics are forever being surprised.

Cynicism's knowingness cheats itself out of true knowing.

Cynics need constant reassurance; first, that their worst doubts about humanity are true and then, of course, that they are not.

Don't let it go to your head;
let it get to your heart.

Time heals old wounds only because there are new wounds to attend to.

Poets are citizen journalists.

Perhaps a midlife crisis is the panic that our
powers may not be equal
to the tasks that still lie ahead.

After asking a question
of the Divine, listen.

Personal effort and responsibility ...
before any talk of Divine assistance.

Half of seeing ourselves in everyone is compassion, the other half is arrogance.

Best not flirt with disaster lest it decides to commit.

For writing that is essential,
from the marrow of our being,
there is never a rush.
Such truths are living entities that –
if forced out prematurely – will be
deformed or worse, stillborn.

In the embrace of tragedy is sublime beauty.

To the trained ear, patience rhymes with hope
rhymes with faith.

There are no *un*chosen people.

Surrendering our will is part of hoping and trusting in mystery beyond our control.

Everything is beautified and seen
for what it truly is, miraculous,
when it catches the Light.

Fire releases our deepest sweetness.

Miracles are everyday occurrences,
recognising them is not.

Artists are only a great longing ...
and some strategically-placed mirrors.

The divisions in our heart prevent us from healing those in the world.

America: the hand that feeds you,
then beats you.

Our most profound prayers hardly reach our lips – they are made with our entire being.

Our wounds are peepholes through which we see the wounds of the world.

Imagine, if we stopped migrating birds at the border and said, 'No, this stretch of sky, sea and land is out of bounds. Can you perch somewhere else, please? Perhaps in your native trees?'

Human perversity: one who suffers a little is able to relate to the suffering of another. Yet, if they suffer too much they helplessly repeat the vicious cycle.

The more we prattle with others the less of a chance we have for a serious conversation with ourselves.

At the heart of every vice sits selfishness, yawning.

Sometimes, Love is biting
your tongue – until it bleeds.

In the spiritual dimension, one cannot produce a masterpiece until becoming one.

How attentive the forces of darkness are, how they rush to fulfil our ill-conceived wishes.

It's not what you know, but what you are.

It's difficult, in times like these,
not to become radicalised –
the question is: will it be
by all-consuming hatred
or compassion?

Anthropologists must also be apologists.

Spirituality occurs at the boiling point of religion, where dogma evaporates.

Bitterness is an insidious disease of the heart.

The answer to the question is
invariably one of the following:
patience, forgiveness, sacrifice,
hope, gratitude, prayer.
In other words, Love.

The poet's notepad is a prescription pad.

If not humility, then humiliation will be
the key to salvation.

The weak in power
must seek to be morally strong.

Before we even begin to consider outer space, first contemplate inner space.

If each of us houses the Divine, then to take another's life is to murder a piece of God.

In matters of the spirit, a little is a lot.

Every war is criminal, some are blasphemous.

If words alone could change the
world, we would not still be
where we are today.
Heal your heart,
the world transforms.

Political activism is not enough;
spiritual revolution is needed.

Sometimes, small heresies
are required for greater faith.

Style: deciding how you want to
interact with the world.

Purity of heart = clarity of perception.

Unlike snakes, venom poisons most those persons who carry it.

Let your secrets be good deeds.

To want or desire nothing of another human,
even expect nothing of the heavens,
this is freedom ... Yet, to burn for union
– one of life's paradoxes.

Confront the abyss before making
peace with groundlessness.

To laugh out of sheer joy might be our most natural and holy state: innocent and wise.

It's not the sin that offends the unrepentant,
but the mirror held up to it.

Ah, the sport of dreams ...
The passes made to us, the goals!

Hallucinating is a sign of intelligence -
it is common to dreaming and AI.

Praise hallows.

Unheeded, pricks of conscience might return
as harpoons of circumstance.

Across millennia, the devil's siren song
remains unaltered: 'Let it all burn!'

Think of the devil as scared and all his counsel
issuing from a place of desperation.

Learn to forgive, countless times,
the way you are forgiven
by your Creator.

Souls can be wed, without ceremony
spirits marry in the ether
vows are taken, wordlessly
love made, bodilessly.

To an independent spirit, the telling of one side of a story makes it easier to sympathise with the other side.

To find out if Love is true, do not simulate it.

A sublime, meaningful existence has been prepared for us – what is required is to pay attention, bear witness, give thanks.

Only those who fully grasp our imperilled existence insist on transformation.

Lies, suppression of truth and lack of trust are breeding grounds for conspiracy theories.

No revolution is successful without evolution.

If we look at ourselves deeply,
we pardon others.
If we look even deeper,
we realise there are no others.

In silence we honour the unsayable.

An affinity exists between extremes:
they are equidistant from moderation.

Artists are like mystics. They lower their
buckets deep into our communal well to
retrieve what we thirst for.

Mercy is the Divine in us.

Because nothing is free,
ask of your actions: At what cost?

We can most be ourselves around those
whose eyes are trained inward.

If we remain underwater long enough,
we don’t drown, we develop gills.

There are probably as many kinds
of smiles as there are silences.

Remembering how far we've come
is a spur to how far we can go.

Accept setbacks, expect miracles.

Mercy is, unfathomably, greater than justice.

Justice keeps score;
mercy cancels the balance.

Worldly people speak of the value of having a network of connections. Spiritual people understand the necessity of connection to the One.

Living without skin is living without sin.

Our metaphysical eyes are expert at
collapsing distances – seeing through
the apparent to the infinite.

Where there is Love, there can be criticism.

Envious of natural disasters,
humans create their own.

Self-consciousness: a weed in the garden of self-awareness.

Unanswered prayers are, nevertheless, imperishable. They are merely deposited into some eternal account, accumulating interest.

Everything beautiful is in need of our protection.

Gaza is a child
with an amputated arm,
still trying to make music ...

In the face of violent reality, try to remain
moon-drunk and feathered.

There is a time for running away
and a time for returning Home.

Eye contact: how souls catch fire.

We all have disabilities.
The difference is that some of us
must reveal ours, while others
must conceal theirs
to be treated with mercy.

Revelation: the discovery of
a new application for an old truth.

To encounter the vanity of our times, search
for #spiritual or #wisdom on Instagram.

The mind, an erogenous zone, is helpless
before those who stimulate it.

If we allow them, we are guided by invisible, benevolent forces.

The mark of authenticity, for poetry,
is surprise – in poet and reader alike.

Truth can be like a large, bothersome fly –
brush it away and it returns buzzing.

Perhaps Hell is a revolving door,
and Heaven is knowing when to get out.

The poet does not address
the active, scattered person
but rather the contemplative
individual seeking wholeness.

We are never alone in our weaknesses; it is only in our strengths that we sometimes are.

Detach from expectations yet trust that
what we give returns to us.

Two things that stain the mind,
long after they have stained the hands:
blood and newspapers.

The small spirit is quick
to misperceive an insult,
the large spirit slow to receive a compliment.

Our past shadows us, sometimes hiding behind our backs and other times entering the room before us.

With despair, as with night-vision, the eyes
soon grow accustomed to the dark.

Life is a time-release capsule granting us only
glimpses of ourselves at a time.

Philosophies, like roadmaps,
are not to be consulted whilst driving.

To hurry pain is to leave a classroom
still in session.
To prolong pain is to remain seated
in a vacated classroom
and miss the next lesson.

Wit: the pounce of a restless insight.

Solitude: the imprisoned soul's
imprisonment of the body.

Solitude tests our weaknesses
and intensifies our strengths,
then pits them against one another.

Hope is more patient than despair
and so outlasts it.

Doubts are shadows, grown bold
in the absence of Light.

In the deep end, every stroke counts.

Treat life as seriously as you would
a dress rehearsal. No more, no less.

All languages are rough translations of our native tongue: Spirit.

Awaking: waiting at the platform of existence
for one's particular train of consciousness
to arrive from faraway lands.

Marrying for looks is like buying books
for their pictures – a good idea
if one cannot read.

Reading a great work is being granted
an audience with a great mind.

If religions are understood as organised love, then hate is heresy.

Mercy is to cover the nakedness of others and stand beside them, naked.

Think of existence as a great love story – every shy creature or timid truth wants to be courted.

True love is the One we keep returning to.

Don't wake a sleepwalker, they say. The same applies to lifelong day-dreamers: children, artists, thinkers, mystics, lovers or revolutionaries.

Love has no off button – even though we may switch stations or turn the volume down.

We only ever love once, though there are a hundred versions of it.

In the same way that love is regenerative medicine, hate is a degenerative disease.

Art is the love we make by
ourselves, says the ego.
Art is the love we make with
an invisible other, replies the spirit.

Those whom life trusts, she tells a secret or two. If they betray her, she is slow to trust again.

Those who speak ill of life do not realise that they only smear their own names.

Social media:
ballroom of dancing consciousnesses.

As we make peace with ourselves,
we become more tolerant
of our faults – in others.

Miracles are proud creatures; they only reveal themselves to those who believe.

Intuition: generous deposits made to our account by an unknown benefactor.

A small curiosity is petty,
but a great curiosity philosophical.

Spiritual fast-food leads
to spiritual indigestion.

History does not repeat itself,
human nature does.

Our wisdom always mocks us
since it knows more than we can.

We are cruellest when we ought to be kindest:
when someone is losing a battle or war
we've waged and won before.

If we do not care for our souls,
we become a burden to others.

It is one of love's curious laws that we only
permit others to love us
to the extent we do ourselves.

If love, as they say, is blind
then lust must be deaf, dumb and blind.

The most consummate actors are too
accomplished on life's stage
to risk exposing themselves on film.

To enter each day with empty
hands, trusting you will
receive what you need –
such is the spirituality of poverty.

Expecting large miracles
prevents us from recognising the
countless small ones granted daily.

Self-image: self-deception.

The regrettable thing about insecurity is how dearly everyone else must pay for it.

Time forbids attachments. Clinging to a particular time is courting madness.

Sacred signs everywhere,
yourself among them.

Idol worship: a perversion of self-worship.

To maintain immaculate speech,
often silence is required.

Narcissism requires keeping a distance from
one's reflection; an inch closer,
and the love spell is broken.

Self is a labyrinth,
at the heart of which sits Spirit,
hoping to be found.

The bigot's crime is twofold: not knowing
others well enough to love them,
and not having enough self-knowledge
to recognise their own hatred.

Every enmity with another is part of our
unfinished work on ourselves;
a free person has no enemies.

If we listen, the air is heavy
with poems, ripe for plucking.

By remembering the light,
we can smile in the dark.

Every day we're offered this world or the next; but one cannot be myopic and farsighted, at once.

We must try not to take our fight with ourselves out into the world.

We suffer from mass logorrhea; memoirs and blogs are twin afflictions of our literary times.

In serving words faithfully, we also serve one another.

The guardian of the riddle
must speak in riddles.

Logical interpretations
are the miracle's modesty.

So long as you trust in anything else,
the miracle shall be withheld.

Radical humility is to entertain the possibility that our worst detractors might be right about us.

To acquire a third eye, one cannot blink.

Fear of success betrays
a greater self-mistrust than fear of failure.

It's easier to be fearless
when we remember that we are deathless.

Only love can heal
the wounds of love.

The great whale hunt of the spirit life
is also pursued in our dreams.

All who are tormented by an ideal
must learn to make an ally of failure.

Our salvation lies on the other side
of our gravest danger.

Unattended temples
are reclaimed by wilderness.

To better see, as darkness falls,
move closer towards the Light.

Every Messiah is reluctant – at least initially.

Intuition asks: What use are two open eyes
when you're in the dark?

Where there are demons,
there is something precious worth fighting for.

Silence and Time are wiser than us.

We do not choose our Work,
we merely consent to it.

Signs of mercy? How we continue to be
rewarded, as we continue to transgress.

Vastness: our only way out of this
narrow-hearted mess …

We are shamed into self-improvement when our transgressions are met with forgiveness and generosity. This is also the foundation of faith.

Paradox: the cloak preferred by profound truths.

There are two ways through: one is fiendish complexity, the other is utter simplicity.

Aphorisms are the sushi of literature.

Rigidity is the need to conclude.
Let the last sentence of your soul
stand open-ended ...

What do we look for in a good book,
painting, music or conversation?
A stretch of runway to take off
and return us to ourselves.

Looking a gift horse in the mouth
is the human condition.

Everything we do here matters, elsewhere.

Without the generosity of the poor,
the rich would surely perish.

Pandemics are also tests of
emotional intelligence.

The paradox of success in life
is to be aware of your vices, not your virtues.

Much of what passes for antisemitic,
these days, is antisemantic.

Prayer is also anesthesia,
so we can cut deeper,
and clean out our wounds.

No respite in the garden without,
first, struggle in the wilderness.

The master and the novice are not permitted
to make the same mistakes.

Inspiration speaks in fits and starts – revealing
to us only what is necessary at the time.

When in doubt,
meditate upon your wound.

To transcend Time, transcend Self.

Silence is, sometimes, the charitable answer.

True solitude is not lonely,
it is companionable.

The prayers most likely to be answered are selfless ones that we make for others.

As in the physical realm, so in the spiritual – it takes one moment of inattention to slip and fall.

The question, now, is:
Who will defend Israel from itself?

Recognise the warped virtues
wrapped within your vices.

Free speech is not an absolute good,
nor is censorship an absolute evil.

The danger of cynicism is getting what you believe in: nothing.

From what you have,
create what you have not –
the poem teaches the poet.

You cannot bury pain
and not expect it to grow roots.

Pity the rational mind.
It would sooner accept a believable lie
than an incredible truth.

The heart is patient with the mind
because it knows better.

Optimist and pessimist each shut an eye
to tell their half-truths.

Wars are the side-effects of nationalism.

Nothing is without its price,
free-thinking included.

If there is someone we might ask forgiveness from, then there is no one we can deny forgiveness to.

To the humble spirit, criticism
is cause for self-contemplation.

The best type of censorship
is self-censorship – aka morality.

Complete honesty is the luxury of the
utterly good, or the utterly shameless.

Wings are, always, on loan.

Poems are like bodies – a fraction of their power resides in their skin. The rest belongs to the spirit that swims through them.

When we think we are stealing from life's fleeting pleasures, we are stealing from our own eternal joy.

The ascetic does not deny pleasure; they shun the coarse, in favour of the exalted.

The more closely we listen to ourselves, the more likely we are to overhear others.

If our hearts should harden
and turn to ice,
we must try, at least,
not to blame the weather.

The ascetic ideal speaks thus:
indulge, and forgo Vision.

To mate with the sublime, sublimate.

Said a poem to a poet: Can I trust you?
Is your heart pure to carry me?
Are your hands clean to pass me on?

If you wish to be heard,
speak gently.
The same holds true
in speaking to ourselves.

For the sake of a good line
a poet, like a comedian,
must be willing to risk everything.

When the life of a poet is a poem,
the poet becomes a mystic.

Numbness is a spiritual malady,
true detachment its opposite.

To receive what we need most,
we must first give it away.

If we care for ourselves,
we may turn our pain into a gift for others.

We steal from ourselves when we share an
idea, or a feeling, before it has ripened.

Why announce to the world
your few good deeds, when you hide
your many bad ones – even from yourself?

Spiritual initiation:
knowledge received intravenously.

We can still become who we once were.

To write is to bow is to pray.

Bow so low and you kiss the sky.

The problem with being full of yourself is that you cannot fill up with much else.

To evolve means we've been listening.

If we ask life for favours,
we must be prepared to return them.

Just as mysteriously as spiritual favours are
granted, so they may also be revoked.

The master of darkness
is a student of the Light.

Unlike prose, poetry can keep its secrets.

Poetry is what we say to ourselves
when there's nowhere to hide.

Poetry is the distance
between us and our pain.

How we address our pain
can help us prolong or overcome it.

We scramble the first half of our lives
to assemble a self; and in the second half,
if we are wise, to dismantle it.

It's not easy to speak to ourselves –
we must devise ruses, interventions.

Character is what we are in company –
alone we are everyone.

Being frightened by your shadow
and making peace with it
are not mutually exclusive.

Conversation: an encounter
between all that we know
and what we are about to discover.

Conversation, there's nothing like it –
except silence.

Mysticism is the disappearing act
that takes a lifetime.

To become a mystic is not impossible;
one must only endure being a beggar,
mad and dead.

Heaven save us from
tragic seriousness;
teach us to play, divinely.

It is possible to subsist entirely
on a diet of honey and wine,
also known as poetry and mysticism.

When the Muse is silent, confess ignorance.

Art alters the artist and, in time,
recreates them in its own image.

Strange, how our weaknesses can
be strengths in disguise
and vice versa.

Reality is a rose of a thousand petals.

A poem arrives like a hand in the dark.

There are no shortcuts to transcendence.

Inhibitions might be
the handmaidens of conscience.

When we blame others, we miss the opportunity to blame ourselves.

Practise preparedness.

Tattoo: graffiti on a masterpiece.

Does the contemporary prevalence of 'life coaches' mean Life can no longer be relied upon to do her job?

The play of ideas is eternal.
We merely shuffle onstage and off
to introduce them to one another.

The contemplative life is not a passive one.

A good listener helps us overhear ourselves.

We're here to pass around the ball of light,
while keeping our fingerprints off it.

Each time we betray our conscience, we strangle an angel. Yet it's not certain we are allotted an infinite supply of winged pardons.

Know your Muse, and its diet.

Things are at their most comfortable
before they collapse –
be they armchairs or relationships.

No matter how we dream or scheme,
being born is always a surprise.

In life, as in love,
graceful leave-taking is the epitome
of gratitude.

About the author

Yahia Lababidi, Lebanese-Egyptian of Palestinian descent, is the author of twelve collections of poetry and prose. Lababidi's latest work, *Palestine Wail* (Daraja Press, 2024), is a lament for the ongoing genocide of Palestinians and a plea to heal our wounded world. His aphorisms and poems have gone viral and are read in classrooms, at peaceful protests and in religious services as well as at international literary festivals.

Lababidi has also contributed to news outlets, and literary and cultural institutions throughout the USA, Europe and the Middle East, including Oxford University, Pearson Education, PBS NewsHour, NPR and HBO as well as ABC Radio.

Praise for Yahia Lababidi's work

Yahia Lababidi's work is characterised by a contemplative tone in line with Rumi ... Lababidi is a Muslim voice for peace, celebrating the wisdom in ancient traditions and pointing out the ridiculous in the rush and cynicism of contemporary life. Drawn to the mystic tradition, he often refers to the virtues and fruits of silence and writes that his aphorisms 'respect the wisdom of silence by disturbing it, briefly'. Perhaps an age as thoughtless and noisy as our own requires a whole book full of them.
— *Plough Quarterly*

Like every divine utterance, the only way to honour Lababidi's work is to memorise it. I'm starting today. I am moved, touched and remade by his words, sincerity and truth beyond measure. This has not been an easy time for the world, these words heal.
– Robert Inchausti, author of *The Way of Thomas Merton*

[Lababidi's] aphorisms exhort us to pay attention, believe we can make a difference, keep our hearts open in the face of pain, take responsibility for our actions, avoid ego and do the hard work that comes with sticking to ideals.
— Elizabeth Flock, *PBS NewsHour*

Yahia Lababidi punctures our little worlds of self, and when we peer through each pinprick we see a cosmos, a new one each time.
— Kevin Hart, author of *Poetry and Revelation*

Egyptian-born Lababidi is a poet, aphorist, essayist and mystic. He is steeped in the traditions of Western philosophy but comes from a world where the desert reminds you constantly that you are surrounded by a vast inimical emptiness; the ancient Christian hermits used to sit in the Egyptian desert because from there you could place a toll-free call to Paradise … Although it may seem contradictory to say so, the mystic is a person in conversation; everything in him burns toward that conversation.
— Douglas Glover, author of *Savage Love*

Like a modern Guru, Yahia Lababidi, with his wise aphorisms, shows us the path from darkness to light, untruth to truth, and mortality to immortality.
— Abhay Kumar, Indian poet and diplomat.

Blaise Pascal, a French mathematician, physicist, inventor, writer, once said, 'I have only made this letter longer because I have not had the time to make it shorter.' It is easy to dump 10,000 words on paper. It is much harder to distil what's worth saying into 10 words. Fortunately for us, Yahia Lababidi has done the hard work of carving out unneeded rock and giving us an exquisite sculpture.
— Anu Garg, American author, speaker, and founder of Wordsmith.org